THE GHOSTLY TALES OF GRANBURY

Published by Arcadia Children's Books
A Division of Arcadia Publishing
Charleston, SC
www.arcadiapublishing.com

First published 2021

Manufactured in the United States

ISBN 978-1-4671-9833-2

Library of Congress Control Number: 2021938353

Images used courtesy of Shutterstock.com; p. 2 xradiophotog/Shutterstock.com.

Spooky America

The Ghostly Tales of Granbury

Brandy Herr

Adapted from *Haunted Granbury* by Brandy Herr

arcadia®
CHILDREN'S BOOKS

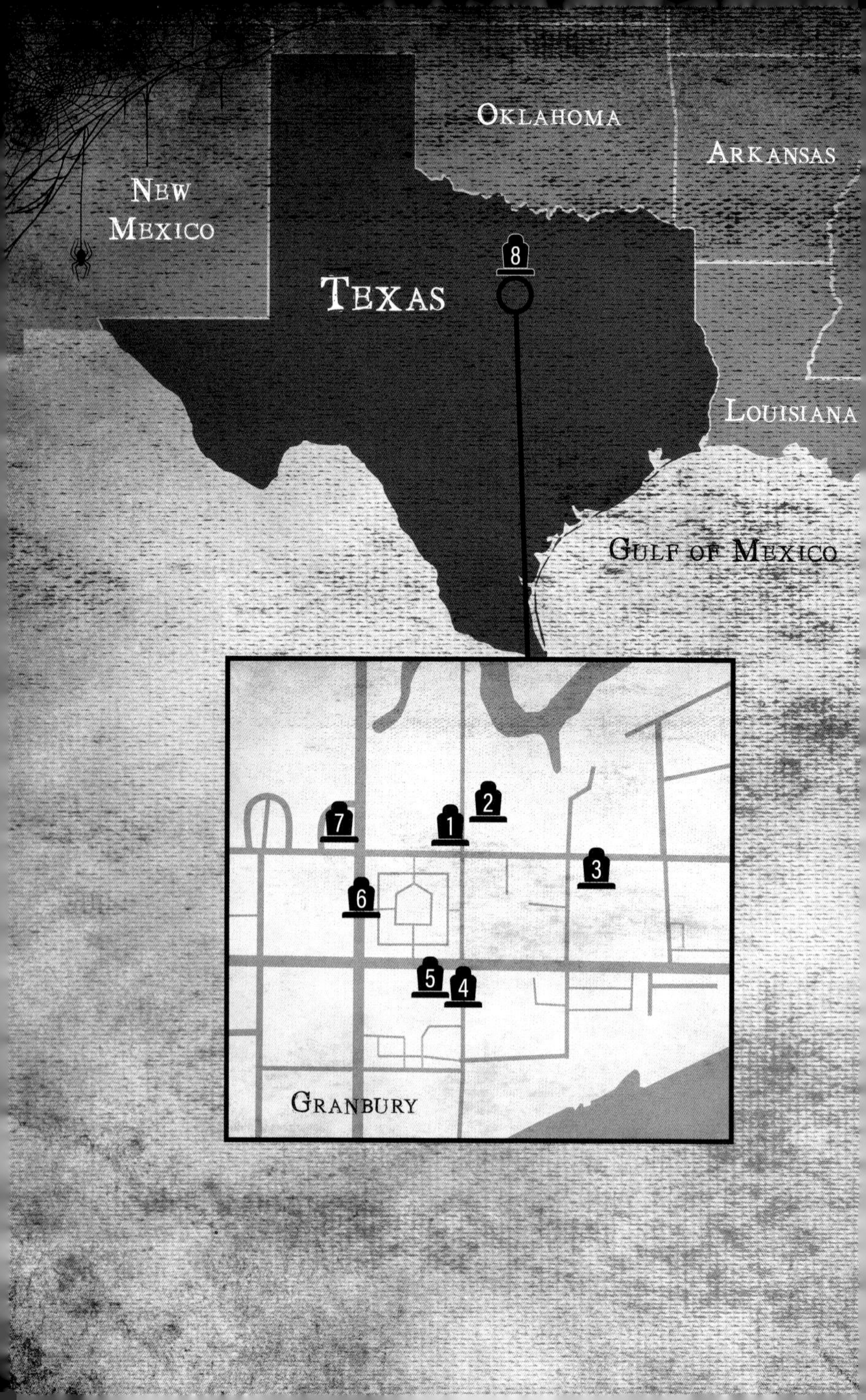

Oklahoma
Arkansas
New Mexico
Texas
8
Louisiana
Gulf of Mexico
2
7
1
3
6
5
4
Granbury

Table of Contents & Map Key

Elevated Water Tower in Granbury

Introduction

Welcome, fearless reader! Journey, if you dare, to the town of Granbury, where Texas history lives. Or, like some say, where Texas history never left.

Built not long after the American Civil War, Granbury has seen its fair share of mystery and mayhem. It has been home to heroes and outlaws, to friends and foes, and of course, to more than its fair share of ghosts.

A stroll around Granbury's historic downtown square will take you right back in time. You can almost see the distinguished gentlemen and ladies of yesteryear mingling with the cowboys and bartenders. Are they just a figment of your imagination? Or something else altogether?

The spooky history of Granbury has intrigued travelers for years, bringing to town tourists, history buffs, and yes, even ghost hunters. What they have encountered could chill even the bravest of readers to their core.

So sit back and enjoy these ghostly tales of Granbury. But beware: you might find the town so eerily charming, you may want to visit soon. But don't say I didn't warn you.

ICE

CHAPTER 1

The Nutt House Hotel

Jesse and Jacob Nutt, along with Thomas Lambert, donated the land that became the county seat of Hood County, the townsite of Granbury. Much more than just a funny last name, the Nutt brothers and their families were very important in founding the town that we know and love today.

In 1893, the Nutt brothers built what is now known as the Nutt House Hotel as their mercantile shop at 119 East Bridge Street on the northeast corner of the Historic Downtown Square. The Square is the heart of Granbury, filled with shops and restaurants, and it still delights both tourists and locals with its old-time charm.

Though Jesse and Jacob Nutt were both blind, they didn't let that slow them down. Both stricken with illness at a young age, the brothers learned quickly to adapt to their special needs as they built their successful business. They also had a younger brother, David Lee Nutt, who would help them when they needed assistance from a sighted person. David's granddaughter, Mary Lou Watkins, later opened a restaurant inside the building, and though she died in 2001, it seems she is still running it.

Mary Lou was so important to the town of Granbury. She was a cheerleader during a time when the town really needed some cheering up. In the 1960s, she began to fix up her house along with the Nutt Building, which inspired others in town to do the same. Because of

her, the entire town square is now noted as a historic destination. There is even a statue of her across the street from the Nutt House Hotel, ringing her bell like she loved to do when she ran her restaurant to announce that dinner was on the table.

Mary Lou isn't just seen on the corner, however. Oh, no. Even now, visitors and employees have still seen her walking up the stairs, her hair pulled up into a bun, lifting her long skirt as she makes each careful step.

Other restaurants have come and gone since Mary Lou's time, and employees continue to feel her presence. Cabinet doors open, and water faucets turn on by themselves. The very heavy back door in the kitchen can be heard banging or sometimes even seen flying open, even though it is impossible to open without working the latch!

Coletta Henderson, an employee of a former restaurant inside the Nutt Building, was training a new hire one slow evening. While in the back dining room, they suddenly heard the sound of women's laughter near the front door. Henderson was the only female in the building at the time, and no one had heard the squeaky front door open. The two rushed to the front, ready to apologize to the waiting customers, only to find that no one was there!

However, the Nutt House Hotel, located on the second floor, is where the real fun begins. Though spooky happenings have been reported in just about every room, the most excitement (or the most terror, whichever you prefer) can be found in Room Four, also called the Mary Lou Watkins Suite.

Is there something special about that room, or is Mary Lou just flattered to have a room named after her? It's hard to know for sure.

But odds are if a guest reports any unusual or unexplained activity, they are probably staying in Room Four.

One particular incident that occurred in the room is quite chilling—literally. Two women were staying overnight in Room Four. Around 4:30 in the morning, one of the women woke up with a jolt, with the sensation that someone had been furiously shaking her. However, as she turned her head to the side, she discovered

her companion still in deep slumber beside her. Shaken, she woke her friend up and explained to her what had happened. They lay in the bed, wide-eyed, wondering what was going on. Suddenly, the temperature in the room became icy cold, and loud knocks were heard banging throughout the room. The women knew there was no way they were going back to sleep that night!

Other guests of the hotel have reported hearing voices or footsteps when they knew they were the only visitors there at the time. Their towels would get moved around in the bathroom, the lights would turn on and off, and guests would leave their room with the ceiling fans turned off only to find them turned on at high speed when they return. Sometimes guests even feel like they aren't alone in the bed, and a weight can be felt laying down next to them!

In the upstairs lobby, which just so happens to be right outside the door to Room Four, the hotel innkeeper will lower the wooden blinds in the windows. However, she will later come back to find that the blinds have been raised once more. She would be the only person in the building at the time, so how could window blinds raise on their own?

Mary Lou Watkins was a powerful presence in life, and she still is in death. Because she took it upon herself to renovate both the Nutt House Hotel and her historic home just off the Square, she gave others in town the encouragement they needed to do the same with their buildings. She is credited with almost single-handedly revitalizing the Historic Downtown Square and bringing her beautiful hometown back from the brink of disrepair. Her work in the 1960s helped create the Granbury that we know today, and her lingering spirit continues to attract and astonish visitors. Her stories even helped to inspire the Granbury Ghosts and Legends Tour and the creation of this book! So to Mary Lou, we would like to say, "Thank you, and please stick around for as long as you would like!"

CHAPTER 2

The Historic Hood County Jail

Around the corner from the Nutt House Hotel, lurking just off the Historic Downtown Square, is the Historic Hood County Jail. It is quite possibly the creepiest building in downtown Granbury! With the rusty iron jail cells upstairs, the sheriff and his family lived downstairs, with the sheriff's wife cooking for and tending to the inmates that were imprisoned just above her head. You can even still see writing all over the walls from the prisoners who were locked up there. Add to that the tall front tower built for executions—though it was never actually used—and the small, dank room of solid stone to house the "women and insane" people, and you have yourselves one spooky building!

This jail was built in 1885, and it still housed inmates all the way up until 1978. That's almost one hundred years' worth of people who have had the displeasure of being locked up within the walls of the jail, some of them friendly, some of them not so much.

The most popular spirit to linger within the walls of the old jailhouse is that of a Native American man known as Joe. Bobbie Jordan, the former director of the Granbury Chamber of Commerce, had plenty of encounters with Joe. Before the jail became the museum that it is today, it housed the chamber offices. When

Jordan would work in her downstairs office, all alone in the building, she would often hear the sound of footsteps walking slowly down the stairs and into her room. He would then settle into a corner of the room to keep her company. She could always feel his presence, "almost like I could see him, but I never did," she once remarked. However, Jordan had one run-in with Joe that got just a little more personal than she would have preferred.

One evening, Bobbie Jordan was working late to meet a deadline. As she sat at her desk, typing away furiously, she felt Joe's familiar presence enter the room. There was just one problem: this time, he wasn't walking to his familiar corner. The footsteps approached Jordan at her desk. Closer, and then closer still. Suddenly, she felt "as if a thick, misty cloud enveloped [her] entire body."

Joe was sitting on her lap!

Jordan leapt away from her desk and ran home in her stockings, not even pausing to pick up her shoes as she fled.

But how do we know this spirit is named Joe? There is no record of him in the books. It came down to a group of ladies touring the building while their husbands were at a fishing tournament in town. They became fascinated with the ghostly stories they heard on their tour, and one woman stepped forward, claiming to be an automatic writer. An automatic writer is a medium, or a person who can communicate with spirits, and allows the spirit to use their hand to write out messages to the living. Joe used this woman to tell the others his name and to explain that he was a Native American who had become separated from his tribe.

The ladies then asked him if he would come join them. As soon as they asked, he came right down the stairs, allowing everyone to feel his presence. They decided this must mean that he is lonely without his tribe and simply seeking out company wherever he can find it, even if he does have a bit of a boundary issue!

Joe is far from being the only spirit that resides in the old jailhouse, however. In fact, so much paranormal activity has occurred within those walls that it would be impossible to name each and every one of the spirits. That hasn't stopped ghost hunters from trying, though.

The Historic Hood County Jail Museum has quickly become the most popular location in town for paranormal research groups. At least once a month, it is not unusual to see ghost hunters setting up their equipment and searching for spirits. If you go into this old jailhouse looking for ghosts, you are almost guaranteed to find them! In fact, one paranormal team even said that they investigate there so much not because they are trying to find something new, but because they know the place is so active, they use it as a base to test their new equipment!

The most common piece of evidence found by paranormal investigators comes in the form of an electronic voice phenomenon, or EVP. Many times, when a spirit is speaking to you, you can't hear their voice with your ear alone. It takes too much energy for a ghost to manifest itself enough to be detected by living humans. Because of this, ghost hunters will bring in audio recorders to capture EVPs. The ghost can then tap into the energy from the electronic device to record their responses. Of course, this means that much of an investigation is nowhere near as exciting as what you see on TV. It's a lot of talking to the air and just hoping that the air talks back.

One particular paranormal investigator caught some compelling EVPs, but it appears she may have also caught a bit more. Chrystal Ramadan was investigating the jailhouse with her team when she discovered a poem written on the wall of the jail cell by a former inmate:

In the silence of a prison cell,
Your thoughts of the events that's led
you here come and go
And you ask yourself why!
Only then do you realize that the
course of history can't be changed,
only sidetracked.
For your destiny is forever in
forward motion.
So let your time here be short; Your
thoughts long lived; And Remembered.
Stephen Lee
Alias The Poet 9-26-78

Ramadan read these words aloud, and she felt a sudden shift in the air, as if someone had become very angry. They then received an EVP recording of an old man saying, "Oh, shut up!" Was this Stephen Lee, angry that he thought she was mocking his work? Or was it a critic, someone with a dislike for poetry?

Another popular technique used by investigators is the "flashlight trick." Using this technique, ghost hunters encourage the spirit to use the energy in the flashlight's batteries to turn the light on and off in response to their questions.

Ramadan asked the spirit, "Is your name Stephen?" Her face was suddenly bathed in light as the flashlight turned itself on in response.

Ramadan decided to take it a bit further, provoking the ghost to get a reaction. She called out, "I don't believe you are here!"

Stephen got mad. The investigators suddenly heard furious banging all over the cell walls. One young girl that came along with the team suffered a painful scratch at the hands of

an unseen entity. Now Ramadan got mad, too. "You are a jerk for scratching this poor girl!" she called out.

It seems Stephen then decided to pick on someone his own size. After the investigation, the spirit attached itself to Ramadan and followed her home. She soon began to suffer mysterious setbacks, both in her health and her personal life. Since then, she has managed to recover and move on, but not without a long moment of struggle. Sometimes spirits just don't like to be criticized.

CHAPTER 3

The Langdon Center

Just off the Square at 308 East Pearl Street sits a stately old home known as the Langdon Center, named for Dora Lee Langdon, a patron of the arts who left money in her will for the building to become a cultural center. It is also known historically as the Gordon House, as it was home to the Gordon family when it was first built. It houses art exhibits and music lessons and maybe something more.

Alonzo Peyton Gordon, A.P. for short, had the house built in 1882. He lived there while he owned a popular store and saloon just down the street. In fact, it's even believed that he was the boss of a very infamous and legendary Granbury resident, but let's save that for a later chapter, shall we?

A.P. Gordon is still known to stick around in his old home. It's not uncommon for people to catch a man in a white shirt and black pants out of the corner of their eye, but when they turn to face him, he has completely disappeared.

Langdon Center staff will be working in their office on the second floor when they hear the front door open and close, followed by footsteps slowly creeping up the stairs. The staff will stop to listen. Creak . . . creak . . . and then nothing. The footsteps stop, never making it past the third step of the staircase.

A man as popular as A.P. Gordon surely had quite a lot of visitors in his day. Even though he is no longer living, that hasn't changed. Employees at the Langdon Center often report hearing the sound of the front doorbell ringing. Normally, that wouldn't be unusual, except the doorbell has been broken for many years. Perhaps the phantom staircase walker was one of Gordon's guests, impatient that no one was answering his ring.

For those living visitors interested in interacting with ghosts, there is another spirit residing at the Gordon House that steals everyone's hearts. Little Audrey Gordon, A.P.'s granddaughter, passed away at the age of five in 1908. Since then, she has remained at the Gordon House, enjoying the music from the lessons and recitals and playing with the children who come through whether they want her to or not.

Children in 1908 were just like the children of today. They loved to laugh and joke and even play pranks. Today, students of the music lessons held at the Langdon Center have reported hearing the laugh of a small child. Sometimes they would open the door of their rehearsal room to find that it was locked and that they were trapped inside! Luckily, Audrey was simply playing a game, so they were never trapped for very long. Kids would be heard exclaiming to their parents, "You'll never guess what Audrey did to us this week!"

The stories of Audrey's shenanigans attracted the attention of ghost hunting group Research and Investigation of the Paranormal, or RIP. RIP has investigated the Langdon Center a few times now, and their findings have been both astonishing and chilling.

Little children, whether alive or not quite, love an audience, and Audrey is no exception!

When RIP's cameras come out, she comes to play. On their first investigation, the group brought a guitar, since they had heard that she loves listening to music. Three members entered the home for a "sweep."

In ghost hunter speak, a sweep is when a small group of investigators enter the building to try to interact with the spirits and capture evidence. The rest of the investigators stay outside to rest or keep an eye on the monitors. If you have too many people going in at once, it can be harder to know if the noise you hear is coming from someone living or dead. Plus,

investigations can go for hours throughout the whole night, so breaks are important! So teams perform sweeps, rotating the members every hour.

For this particularly fateful sweep, the team members entering the home were Brandon Stephens, Tyler Solomon, and Brandy Herr.

Stephens played the guitar while Solomon and Herr sang along, all having a fun time in the hopes that Audrey would want to join in. At one point, Stephens stopped playing the guitar to hand a flashlight to Solomon. While the three investigators heard nothing at the time, later upon reviewing the recording, a very clear voice was heard during that silent moment. A little girl, desperate to keep the party going, cried out, "Don't stop playing, Brandon!"

Audrey does love her music. On another sweep, Greg Stephens, the leader of RIP, entered the home to play the guitar as well. After strumming a few notes, he paused. That was when another voice recording was caught: "Can you do it again? Can you?" He later asked Audrey if she enjoyed listening to people play the piano in the house. His question was met on the recording by a high-pitched, enthusiastic "Yeah!"

Audrey loves music so much, she is willing to brave the dreaded cooties in order to listen. RIP brought a ten-year-old junior investigator named Zachary to join them, hoping Audrey might be more likely to come out to play if a child is present. Greg Stephens coached Zachary, telling him, "Make sure to keep quiet and really listen hard. See if Audrey might say something to you. Maybe she wants to come play!" At this point on the recording, investigators heard a little voice respond, "I don't like boys!" You could practically envision her little nose curling up in disgust!

Audrey managed to push her dislike aside, however, when Zachary began to play the piano. He attempted to teach himself how to play "Mary Had a Little Lamb." He found himself growing more and more frustrated as his fingers hit wrong key after wrong key. Finally, after what seemed like hours of agonizing practice, Zachary managed to plunk out exactly the right tune. At this exact moment, heard on the audio recording, is a young girl's excited cry.

"Yay!"

Well, boys may be smelly, at least to five-year-old girls, but Audrey knows good music when she hears it!

If there is anything Audrey loves more than music, it's attention. Because of this, the Langdon Center is often one of the most popular stops along the Granbury Ghosts and Legends Tour. Tour guests love the chance to interact with Audrey, and Audrey loves it just the same. During one investigation with RIP, Audrey was asked, "Do you like it when the ghost tour comes by here?" On the recording came the sly, almost mischievous reply, "Yeeeaaahhh."

It's always helpful when one of a ghost tour's most popular personalities also happens to be a fan. Tour guests love taking pictures of the building in the hope that Audrey will appear, and they are often rewarded with photos of orbs and other unexplained weirdness. One particular photo taken by a past tour guest, however, is enough to turn your blood to ice.

The day after an otherwise uneventful tour, the tour guide received an urgent phone call from a guest on the tour, Miranda Scott, her voice breathless with excitement. "I got something! I got something," she proclaimed.

As the rest of the group moved on from the Langdon Center to continue the tour, Miranda held back to snap some pictures. After the photo shoot was finished and she decided to catch up to the tour, she called out, "Bye, Audrey!" She then took one last picture.

In this final photo, staring out the window, is the clear face of a young girl. Looking much like she does in her Sunday school class photo, Audrey's haunted eyes peer from her pale face, her dark hair pulled up into a little curly pigtail on either side of her head. Oh yes, Audrey does enjoy attention, indeed. She's just looking for someone to come play with her!

CHAPTER 4

137 East Pearl Street

A.P. Gordon's home is located just a couple blocks from his old saloon and mercantile store at 137 East Pearl Street. However, there appears to be other spirits that prefer to linger there, including one of Granbury's most famous, who will be introduced in the next chapter.

The most famous spirit to make her presence known at this building is a woman called "the Lady in Red." The Lady in Red was the owner of another business on the upstairs floor of Gordon's building, and it seems she still believes she is in charge. Her antics have been described as mischievous at best, but sometimes they can be downright dangerous!

Some people tend to be quite protective of their business and property, and the Lady in Red is no exception. If she doesn't like a change being made to her building—and she usually doesn't like changes being made to her building—she will not stay quiet!

Home to a restaurant for over thirty years, the building has seen its fair share of changes,

both in the people and the structure. The Lady in Red has been known to play with and annoy the people that come through, at least when she's in a good mood. One particular longtime employee, Linda Wark, has practically formed a special bond with the Lady.

Spirits can be excellent mimics, making you believe that you heard a specific person's voice when that person is nowhere to be found. The Lady in Red has been known to call out the names of visitors and employees while using Wark's voice, though Wark is not even within earshot.

If that doesn't get her enough attention, the Lady in Red simply raises the volume. When a customer's order is ready to be picked up, the employees use a microphone to call out their number. This microphone will only work if the button is pressed. There have been times, when not a single person is near the pick-up window, the microphone will somehow turn on, and from the loudspeaker, maniacal screaming will be heard. It's enough to make even the most hardened skeptic drop his fork in fear.

Sometimes being heard just isn't enough for the Lady in Red. If busting your eardrums doesn't get the attention she seeks, she might just resort to stealing your food. One hungry customer retrieved his food from the pick-up window and placed it on the table near the front. He then walked to the drink station to fill his cup of coffee. Upon his return to the table, he couldn't believe his eyes. All of his food, plate and all, was missing!

The customer turned, stunned, to see an empty restaurant, with no other living person that could have played such a prank. He then asked Linda Wark about his missing food, and she stepped in to help him search. Finally, after moving the furniture, they discovered the location of the poor man's stolen lunch: underneath the booth in the corner on the floor!

Just think, these antics are just the tricks the Lady in Red plays when she *isn't* angry. When she does get angry, watch out!

A large remodeling effort took place many years ago to replace the wooden boards of the outside sidewalk with concrete. This was enough to send the Lady in Red into such a fit of rage that employees were almost knocked out! Pots, pans, and other kitchen utensils were sent flying through the air, narrowly missing the living occupants of the building. As Wark said, "You would either duck or get hit!"

There is one particular person that the Lady in Red had her eye on, however. If Wark was somehow an uneasy ally with the spirit, this other person had certainly gotten on her bad side.

The Lady in Red gets her name from the dress she is commonly seen wearing. Children, especially, tend to see her, standing on the staircase that leads to the second floor, her hand

resting on the banister, her hip jutted to the side with attitude. She is seen wearing a large black hat over her blonde hair, and of course, a long red dress. A mural painted on the wall of the restaurant in the 1990s pays tribute to the Lady in Red by including her image in the painting. But, as they say, everyone's a critic.

While the artist worked on the mural late one evening, she decided to listen to some music. She turned the radio on and climbed the ladder to begin her work. As soon as she reached the top of the ladder, the radio volume suddenly turned down very low. Puzzled, the muralist climbed back down the ladder, turned up the volume, and then climbed back up to begin working once more. Once again, you guessed it—the radio turned back down as soon as she reached the top.

Convinced there was some sort of glitch causing interference, the artist gave a frustrated sigh and retreated back down the ladder to turn the radio up for the third time. This silliness continued for several more cycles, with the volume always turning down the moment the artist reached the top of the ladder. Finally, Linda Wark arrived to the rescue.

Wark never did put up with the Lady in Red's misbehavior, and this evening was no exception. She called out sternly, "Stop messing with the radio!"

That did it. The radio was quickly forgotten as the Lady in Red turned her fury to the table near the front of the restaurant. The salt and pepper shakers began banging up and down on the table before being angrily thrown against the window, over and over again. After what seemed like an eternity, with Wark and the artist powerless to do anything but stand and watch in stunned silence, the Lady in Red lost her energy, and the shakers were lowered back to the table.

But if you think that was the last of the Lady in Red's fight with the muralist, think again. Perhaps if she couldn't annoy or frighten her, a more direct approach would do it.

On another evening, the muralist was finishing her shift and ready to head home for the night. She had made great progress in the painting, and she wanted to get some rest and freshen up for her next day of work. Her work area had been cleaned, and now all she had to do was put her paintbrushes away. There was just one problem: she couldn't find her paintbrushes anywhere!

How could a painter lose her paintbrushes? She searched her area and all around the restaurant, but not one paintbrush could be found. Wark helped her search as well but came up just as emptyhanded. Why would anyone want to steal twenty-five used paintbrushes? Finally, exhausted, she gave up for the night, vowing to return the next day to try her search once more.

The next day, Wark arrived for work bright and early in the morning. As she unlocked the front door, an unexpected touch of color caught the corner of her eye. She turned her head to the potted ficus tree outside on the sidewalk. There, buried in the dirt around the tree, bristles first with only a small section of each handle poking

through the soil, were all twenty-five of the artist's paintbrushes.

It looks like the Lady in Red was not too happy about how she was being painted in that mural. Like I said, when it comes to art, everyone's a critic!

CHAPTER 5

The Granbury Opera House

Okay, I suppose I have been teasing you long enough. Now it's time to talk about the most famous haunting in Granbury.

In 1865, a man named John Wilkes Booth assassinated President Abraham Lincoln at Ford's Theater in Washington, DC. He jumped from the balcony after doing the deed, breaking his leg and yelling, "*Sic semper tyrannis*!" (Latin for "thus always to tyrants!")

He then ran off, only to be found later in a barn in Virginia, where he was killed. Or was he?

Eyewitness accounts of Booth's death in the Virginia barn describe the man killed to have had red hair and freckles. This does not match Booth's appearance, who had dark hair. Legend has it that another man was killed in that barn, allowing Booth to escape capture. He then traveled to Texas, hoping to stay at the home of a relative in Glen Rose. When his relative learned the truth of what he had done, she quickly kicked him out of her home, and he moved along to Glen Rose's neighboring town, Granbury.

Upon his arrival in Granbury, legend has it that John Wilkes Booth took the name of John St. Helen and tended bar at the saloon owned by A.P. Gordon. Now remember, this is all purely legend. There is no hard evidence to back up these claims. However, there are some interesting tidbits about John St. Helen that just might make you raise your eyebrow.

Granbury residents noted that St. Helen walked with a distinct limp, as if he had broken his leg sometime in the past. Hmmm, sound familiar? St. Helen was also quite the character, often quoting Shakespeare with a dramatic flair. Did I mention that John Wilkes Booth had been a Shakespearean actor?

One day, John St. Helen became very sick. He found himself on what he thought was going to be his deathbed. He decided that now would be the perfect time to confess. In the room at the time were A.P.'s brother F.J. Gordon and an attorney from Tennessee named Finis Bates. According to Bates, these were St. Helen's exact words: "I am dying. My name is John Wilkes Booth, and I am the assassin of President Lincoln. Get the picture of myself from under the pillow. I leave it with you for my future identification. Notify my brother, Edwin Booth, of New York City."

John St. Helen also told F.J. Gordon where he could find the weapon that had killed President Lincoln. After following St. Helen's instructions, Gordon found it easily. Even to this day, it's believed to be somewhere with the Gordon family.

The story doesn't end there, however. Oh no, it's about to get much weirder: John St. Helen, much to his own surprise, enjoyed a full recovery from his illness! However, this new development caused a bit of a snag in his plans. He realized that when he thought he was about to die, he just might have said a little too much. Well, now that he was no longer near death, St. Helen found he had a new will to live. So he quickly fled from Granbury, and that was the last anyone heard from John Wilkes Booth or John St. Helen.

At least it was, until years later when another man named David George, who lived in Enid, Oklahoma, entered the scene and made the confession that *he* was actually John Wilkes Booth after having escaped from Granbury. It seems that the guilt over what he had done and the fear of living in hiding had finally become too much for him. After relieving himself of his burden, the man claiming to be John Wilkes Booth ended his own life. Upon the discovery of his body, Booth was then mummified and joined a travelling circus, where he became a star attraction.

Yes, you read that right. John Wilkes Booth went from a presidential assassin to an actual mummy! I hope you weren't looking forward to seeing it in person, however. The mummy mysteriously disappeared many years ago and hasn't been seen since. The Case of the Vanishing Mummy!

So where does the Granbury Opera House fit in with this story? John Wilkes Booth was such a fan of the theater, and the opera house is located directly next door to the saloon where St. Helen worked, so it only makes sense that he would still want to hang around there.

Unexplained visions of people who are not really there have been reported throughout the years, and a seat in the balcony will move up and down as if someone is sitting there. One time, in 1976, both occurred at the same time!

The theater company was performing a dress rehearsal for its upcoming show when, to the actors' surprise, a Granbury police officer walked through the back door and interrupted them. He was very concerned over seeing an unknown gentleman enter the front door of the theater and wanted to know who he was. The crew was perplexed. The front door was locked, they explained to the officer. No one could have entered through there—no one living, that is. At that exact moment, the seat in the balcony popped suddenly up, as if someone had been sitting there and stood to make a quick exit. Just to be sure, the police officer and his partner made a sweep of the building, finally confirming that no one else was there besides the cast and crew, and certainly no one was in the balcony. Perhaps John Wilkes Booth had simply wanted to watch the rehearsal and was startled when he had been discovered!

The most interesting piece of evidence came from the paranormal show *Ghost Lab*. The Klinge brothers performed an investigation of the Granbury Opera House in 2009 as part of their program for the Discovery Channel. They captured all sorts of interesting and bizarre

evidence, such as an unexplained blob caught by one of their motion-activated cameras set up overnight near the stage. The camera was set to only record if something physical appeared in front of it. Something physical appeared, all right, but no one can tell what it is! Crew members on the show reported seeing people moving between the seats, including a man in a wide-brimmed hat. One film crew assistant even had his backpack ripped off his body. He refused to go back inside the building after that.

But it was one piece of audio that really stole the show. Brad Klinge brought with him a replica of the weapon used to assassinate President Lincoln. He stood on the stage and waved it around while yelling and taunting John Wilkes Booth, challenging him to make his presence known. It worked. On the recording, a very clear voice responded, "Yes, I'm John Wilkes Booth!"

Now, that is the version of the audio you can hear on the show. However, the actual recording was just a little bit different. It seems Booth had had enough of the taunting, because his actual response was, "Yes, I'm John Wilkes Booth, you . . . "—well, let's just say the last word was not a very nice name to call someone.

The spirit of John Wilkes Booth has been known to wander from time to time. Years ago, a man was spotted inside the opera house lobby by members of the opera company. This man was described as looking exactly like photos they had seen of John Wilkes Booth. No one but the opera company was supposed to be inside the theater at the time, so they cried out, "Hey! What are you doing here?"

The man was startled and ran out the door. Members of the opera company chased after him, following down the street. At the end of the block, the man turned and ran in the front door of an empty restaurant that was boarded up at the time. Knowing there was no way for him to escape the closed building, they ran in, expecting to catch him. But when they entered

the building, they were completely alone. That was much more of a ghostly encounter than just a passing glimpse of movement!

Will we ever know for sure if the spirit of John Wilkes Booth still lingers at the Granbury Opera House? Probably not. But the mystery is all part of the fun!

CHAPTER 6

The West Side of the Square

As if one little ghost girl wasn't creepy enough, Granbury actually has two. Hold onto your seats, though. Because this next little ghost girl has one very distinct feature that's much more terrifying than little Audrey Gordon. This ghost girl doesn't have a face.

There are two versions to the story of how "the Little Faceless Girl" came to be. Either way, it is believed to have occurred sometime in the early 1900s, and it involves a circus. Some people believe that this little girl was with the circus and accidentally got left behind. Forced to wander the streets and fend for herself, things didn't go so well for her. Other people believe that the little girl was actually watching the circus parade down Houston Street from a window upstairs when she got a little too excited and fell.

While we may never know what truly happened to her, she remains a well-known presence throughout the shops on Houston Street, located on the west side of the Historic Downtown Square, the opposite side of the Square from the buildings in the previous chapters. Bouncing back and forth between the buildings, her playful spirit

can be felt by both employees and visitors whether they welcome it or not.

A bookstore that was once located at 124 North Houston Street held a toy section in the back. Inside this toy area stood a display tree covered in plush monkeys that, when their bellies were pressed, let out a loud, shrill shriek. One evening, an employee was all alone in the store. It was past closing time, so the doors were locked, and he was counting the money at the register up front. He felt a sudden chill pass over him. He looked up, startled, but nothing was there. As he lowered his head to continue counting the money, he heard it. Every single monkey on that display tree began shrieking and screaming all at once. While the employee was brave enough not to quit his job right there and then, he did tell his boss that he would no longer work the night shift by himself!

The Little Faceless Girl seems to prefer the area of 112 North Houston Street, however. The employees at Market on the Square, an antique and collectible shop located at that property for many years, encountered the young lady many times. One such employee, Ginny-Rea Urban, formed a connection with the little spirit.

"There were times I would walk in the door, and a burst of energy would hit me that was so powerful, it would cause me to immediately drop anything I was holding," she said. "It felt as if the girl simply had been feeling alone and wanted attention."

It has not been uncommon for those at Market on the Square to experience antics that could only come from a mischievous little child. With so much merchandise on display, the shop became her own personal toy store. Tea sets that had been properly packed away in their wicker baskets the night before were found open and set out when the first employees arrived the next morning. It was as if they had actually interrupted a little girl's tea party! Other toys would be witnessed falling off the shelves as if pushed by unseen hands. She has even been known to bend keys in the back-door lock!

Residents living in the apartments above the shop haven't been spared from encountering the Little Faceless Girl, either. In 1992, a man was visiting his son who lived in one of the apartments. Around 2:00 in the morning, the man woke up to find a young girl standing by the side of the bed. Her hands were folded over her green skirt. She did not speak or move, and he could not make out the details of her face under the gauze-like veil she appeared to wear. Though it can be a bit scary to wake up and find a strange person standing by your bed, the man said he was not frightened and that she felt friendly.

She might be a bit too friendly, however. Another family living in the upstairs apartments sadly lost their beloved dog to the spirit. While nothing appeared to be out of the ordinary to the humans living there, the dog disagreed. Frantically searching and sniffing for something only he could sense, he ultimately plunged over the railing to his death. Was the Little Faceless Girl calling to

him so she could have a playful companion of her own?

So just how did the Little Faceless Girl get her name? Was it just because of one man seeing her wearing a veil? Or was there a much more unsettling cause? Buckle up, because I'm about to tell you.

In the 1980s, Market on the Square was home to one of those popular photography booths where customers could dress up in old-timey clothes and take pictures. One morning, the employees opened the shop to a startling scene. The camera was still sitting on its tripod, like it should have been, yet the tripod had been

dropped down to its lowest setting. No one would have left it like this, because it made the tripod unstable, which could have broken the very expensive camera. The antique chair used as a photo prop had been moved from its normal location, and there was a blue dress draped over the seat.

The employees were stunned. The only people that could have had access to the building overnight were standing right there together, and none of them could understand how this could have happened. They began to tidy up and get ready to open the store, still shaking their heads in puzzlement. Suddenly, one employee glanced into the wastebasket. Lying on the top of the trash was a mysterious photograph. With shaking hands, the employee slowly reached down to pull the photograph out of the bin for a closer look.

The photograph featured a portrait of a little girl sitting on an antique chair, the very chair that had been moved. The little girl was wearing a blue dress, the very dress that had been found draped across the chair. In her lap, the little girl held a bouquet of flowers, and in her hair was a very large bow. Neither the flowers nor the bow had ever been seen inside the store. The flowers were not the concern, however. Neither was the bow. The concern came just below the bow. For though the employees could easily see every detail in the picture, there was no detail in between the hair and the neck, just solid white. The little girl in the picture did not have a face.

CHAPTER 7

The B.M. Estes Building

Anchoring the northwest corner of the Square is the B.M. Estes Building, named for the original occupant, Bevly Memphis Estes. A district attorney and county judge, Estes had his office and store inside the large and imposing brick building that was constructed in 1893. He was a well-loved member of the Granbury community, and he loved the community right back. So much so, in fact, that he didn't want to leave, not even after his death.

The building has housed many businesses throughout the years, including two former clothing stores: Dakota's Kabin and the Clothes Horse. Because the building is so large, these two stores were able to fit comfortably side by side within the same location.

Though other spirits have been experienced there, B.M. Estes remains the most popular apparition. Cindy Hyde, former owner of Dakota's Kabin and the B.M. Estes Building itself, encountered Estes quite often. He seemed to enjoy playing with cards. Hyde would enter the building in the morning, ready to open the store and begin her day. That was when she would notice that the Texas souvenir playing cards that she usually had on display at the front counter would instead be on the floor at the back of the store, stacked neatly on top of one another.

While Estes may have enjoyed the occasional card game, he apparently did not like listening to music while he played. For a time, Dakota's Kabin began selling music, mostly country-and-western compact discs.

To sell these CDs, they installed a special listening wall, complete with headphones where customers could sample the music before deciding which one to buy.

On multiple occasions, both the employees and the customers would look on in awe as the headphones would be flung by unseen hands so furiously, they would rip out of the wall

sockets and fly through the air. One employee was working by herself one day with a clear view of the listening wall. As she watched, the headphones carefully lifted up one by one from their holders, moved forward through the air as if carried, and then dropped with a thud to the floor. The store finally decided to discontinue their listening wall to make room for other merchandise and hopefully give Estes a little more peace and quiet.

Among the western-themed clothing and decor sold at Dakota's Kabin were special cowboy-related "Do Not Disturb" signs for children's bedrooms. These signs, designed to hang from a doorknob, were displayed throughout the store rather than in one central location to help fill in gaps. An employee entered the store one morning to open up and was the first person there for the day. A swift movement caught the corner of her eye. She turned to see one of the door hangers swinging briskly back and forth on the hook. This was puzzling, since nothing else around it appeared to be disturbed. However, she would receive an even bigger shock as she turned her gaze to the rest of the store to discover that every single one of the door hangers throughout the entire store, regardless of where it was hanging, was also swinging wildly, with no other merchandise moving!

B.M. Estes even helped to promote the Granbury Ghosts and Legends Tour. A week before they ran their first tour, the tour owners traveled from door to door on the Square to let the shopkeepers and employees know what they were doing. One of the tour owners entered Dakota's Kabin and approached the counter, saying to the employees, "Hello! I just wanted to let you know that starting next weekend, every Friday and Saturday night, we will be conducting ghost tours around the Square."

The last word had barely escaped her lips when a cowboy boot that had been displayed

on a shelf along the wall went sailing through the air. It landed with a loud thud on the wooden floorboards eight feet away from where it originally sat. The employee laughed and exclaimed, "Well, there's our ghost right there!" Shocked customers were calling their friends from the back of the store. "*This woman was just talking about a ghost tour, and a boot just flew off the wall!*" Some even took pictures of the boot. A ghost tour couldn't ask for better publicity than that!

Cindy Hyde, during the time she owned the B.M. Estes Building, has spent countless hours inside the property, both alone and with others, at all hours of the day and night. In all those hours, she has reported only being truly spooked once.

Late one night, Hyde found herself closing the building alone, as all her employees had left for the evening. She was upstairs, in the area that now houses a hotel and was once B.M. Estes's living quarters for a time. She was on the phone, chatting with a friend, when she clearly heard the back door of the store opening downstairs, followed by the ringing of the bell above the door that alerts employees to someone's presence. Then came the stomping. Thud . . . Thud . . . Heavy footsteps clomped across the floor.

Shaken, Hyde tried to convince herself that it was only one of her employees coming back to pick up something that they had forgotten. She crept down the stairs, making sure to stay on the phone the entire time . . . just in case. Ghosts aren't the only scary nighttime intruders, after all. "Hello?" she called out. "Is anyone there?"

Her question was met with only silence, and her searching was met with only darkness. No one else was in the building except for Cindy Hyde . . . no one living, at least. She remained on the phone as she scurried quickly out of the building and to her car. She still does not know who she heard trudging across her floorboards to this day.

The upstairs level of the B.M. Estes Building is not without plenty of chilling and mysterious stories as well. The hotel on the second story is a popular one for tourists to visit. Because so many people have visited this building, there are plenty of stories where visitors and employees have experienced a bump in the night.

A group of four ladies were staying at the hotel one evening and had been informed that they were the only people who had booked a room. The next morning, one of the ladies descended the stairs and asked Cindy Hyde if someone else had checked in at a later time. Hyde assured her that the four ladies had been the only occupants in the building overnight. The guest explained to Hyde that all four women had heard the sound of another hotel room door opening and closing, along with footsteps and the sound of a suitcase being rolled down the hall. Perhaps the spirit of a former guest who was checking out just a little later than expected?

We've been hearing so much about ghosts that can be scary or intimidating. But sometimes ghosts just want to help.

Sydney Carder, a former employee of the Clothes Horse, was living for a time in the upstairs hotel. One day, she was very sick in bed, her fever dangerously high. A sudden knock at her door interrupted her delirious dreams. She was not expecting any visitors, and she was just too sick to even think about getting up to answer the door. She ignored the knock and sank back into a fitful sleep.

Just as she was about to nod off, a hand touched her leg. She woke with a fright, frantically searching the room to find the person who would have been so bold as to enter her room and touch her. However, there was no other person in the room. She was still quite alone.

Her sickness had raged all day, with no sign of relief. As serious as this illness was, Carder could only assume that she would remain sick for a long time. However, just an hour after her leg was touched by the phantom hand, her fever suddenly broke and she made a full recovery. After that moment, Carder no longer felt any fear from the unexplained occurrences that were experienced within the building. According to her, whatever lives there "is obviously something good."

CHAPTER 8

Jesse James and the Granbury City Cemetery

Okay, I suppose I have scared you enough in these chapters with all this talk of ghosts and spirits. I'm going to let you off the hook now. This next chapter is all about a famous legend, not a ghost. Don't get too relaxed, however. Part of it does still take place in a cemetery.

Before we dive right into the famous legend, let me entice you with a brief yet interesting story. I promise, it will all make sense later. Let me tell you about an arm buried in its own grave at the Granbury City Cemetery.

At the age of thirteen, William Henry Holland fell from a pecan tree and broke his arm. They did all they could to save it, but the doctors had to amputate the arm at three separate spots in order to stop the blood poisoning. The arm is now laid to rest in a special concrete tomb inside the Holland family plot at the cemetery. But just where is the rest of William Henry Holland buried? We'll get to that later.

The most famous person to be buried among the grounds of the Granbury City Cemetery is, without a doubt, Jesse James. Jesse James was one of the most notorious outlaws of all time. He was killed in 1882 by Robert Ford and buried in Missouri. But wait . . . buried in Missouri? Then how is he buried in Granbury, Texas? Well, Missouri is what the history books will tell you. Local legend, however, suggests otherwise.

According to people claiming to be descendants and family members of Jesse James, including a third cousin, Ola Everhard, the death of Jesse James in 1882 was staged as part of a conspiracy theory. Another man named Charlie Bigelow was killed instead, and it is Bigelow who is currently buried in James's Missouri grave. It is believed they even pulled this off with the help of Thomas Crittenden, who happened to be the Missouri governor!

When Thomas Crittenden ran for re-election as governor of Missouri, he made promises that he would end gang activity in the state, including Jesse James's gang. However, while he was making these proclamations, he was not aware that Jesse James himself had been sending in contributions to his campaign, to the tune of $35,000! That would be almost $900,000 today!

The night before Jesse James was killed, according to legend, James met with Crittenden to confess about his contributions. The plan was quickly cooked up to fake James's death, which happened the very next day. He was buried quickly, with no death certificate issued and nothing to prove that he had been killed other than Crittenden's word. It was rumored that Jesse James actually attended his own funeral!

Now that Jesse James was a free man, and Crittenden was able to announce that he had put an end to the vicious James Gang, James changed his name to J. Frank Dalton and got a job working the railroads. This job brought

him to Granbury, where it is said that he met a woman and fell in love. Because of this woman, James moved back to Granbury in 1951 at the age of 103, because this was where he wished to die and be buried.

Oran C. Baker was the sheriff of Hood County at the time of Jesse James's return to Granbury. He befriended this man shortly before James's death. That was when James confessed to Sheriff Baker his true identity.

After Jesse James's death, Sheriff Baker was present during the medical examiner's investigation of his body. Sheriff Baker later described in a newspaper article that he personally counted thirty-two bullet wounds in the body and witnessed a rope burn scar around his neck, burns on his feet, and the end of his index finger was missing. That certainly sounds like someone who led the rough life of an outlaw, doesn't it?

The man Granbury residents believe to be Jesse James died in 1951 and was buried at the Granbury City Cemetery with a headstone that reads, "Supposedly killed in 1882." There

are even small signs along the streets within the cemetery to guide visitors to the grave of this most famous, or infamous, citizen. But wait . . . what about that arm I told you about before? Where does that fit in with the story?

Several years ago, residents and area historians approached the county judge for an exhumation order for Jesse James's grave, meaning they wanted to dig up his grave so they could test his body for DNA. This would put to rest (no pun intended) any doubts as to the identity of the body that people claimed to be the notorious bandit.

After a long, grueling process, the

exhumation order was issued, and the grave was dug up. Any celebration was short-lived, however, as they opened the coffin to discover the body in the grave was missing an arm. Wait, that couldn't be right! Jesse James had both his arms when he was buried! Where did the other one go?

It appears that vandals may have moved the headstones, or perhaps it was something as simple as a typo in the cemetery records, because the man they exhumed was of course not Jesse James but, in fact, William Henry Holland. At the time, Holland had been buried in an unknown grave. His descendants knew where his arm had been buried but never knew where his actual grave was. Because of the attempted exhumation of Jesse James, they were able to give him a proper headstone at his final resting place.

We may never know for sure if Jesse James is actually buried in Granbury or if he is buried in Missouri, as history tells us. Perhaps we don't really want to know. The mystery helps add to the unexplained and otherworldly mystique surrounding the town.

At the very least, between John Wilkes Booth and Jesse James, it shows that Granbury is a great place to visit, whether you're alive or dead!

Afterword

The town of Granbury is shrouded in mystery and intrigue. The voices of the dead whisper through the historic buildings, still leaving their mark. Listen carefully, and you just might hear one of them crying out, desperate to tell you their story.

From infamous outlaws that don't know how to stay dead to former entrepreneurs that just can't give up running the businesses they loved, to eerie little girls that just want someone to play with, when you're in Granbury, you're never alone!

Brandy Herr is the cofounder of the Granbury Ghosts and Legends Tour and co-host of the Spooky Spectacle She earned her Bachelor's degree in public relations and a minor in theatre from Pennsylvania State University. She currently lives in Granbury with her husband.

Check out some of the other Spooky America titles available now!

Spooky America was adapted from the creeptastic Haunted America series for adults. Haunted America explores historical haunts in cities and regions across America. Each book chronicles both the widely known and less-familiar history behind local ghosts and other unexplained mysteries. Here's more from *Haunted Granbury* author Brandy Herr:

For more, visit Brandy's website AuthorBrandyHerr.com, or follow her on Twitter (@AuthorBHerr) and Facebook and Instagram (@authorbrandyherr).